I0164296

Magic

INK

Kristi's Poetry Collection

Black Sapphire

Black Sapphire

MAGIC INK

Copyright © 2015 **Kristi McGee**

Printed in the United States

ISBN-13:978-0692458143
ISBN-10:069245814X

Printed by Createspace 2015
Published by BlaqRayn Publishing 2015

Dedication

This dedication
goes out to
everyone with a
dream.
It is never too
late to live your
destiny...

Black Sapphire

Black Sapphire

Magic

INK

Kristi's Poetry Collection

Black Sapphire

Shattered

Raindrops mixed with
teardrops
In an effort to wash out
the pain
Pencil marks, crumpled
paper, trying to ink away
the stain
Thoughts and memories
swirling round and
round
My heart broken
although it never made a
sound
Shattered pieces of a
broken gem
Splintered sharp and
dripping light
Outwardly masked with
a brilliant smile
My shine.....it's dimming
You'll never notice
Eyes closed
Hands clenched

Ignorance is bliss
Keeping my pain
Strictly in my lane
How many pieces will I
have to gather up??
Bleeding while in
recovery
Bound together by ink
and hope
Prayer is my glue
Now tell me.....

How are you??

Lost

**The sun shone for 10
years
and then the shadows
invaded
her smile was there
but it was changed
her mind young and
articulated
but it was clouded
she was lost to all
yet nobody looked
her pain cloaked
in ponytails and tennis
shoes
her anger shielding her
heart
her terror transcendent
of nightmares into her
waking reality**

**Day in
Day out**

Black Sapphire

Breathe in
Breathe out
Stop!!!!

{Insert Pain Here}

grow older
grow wiser
hide the infestation
with witty retorts
and sly conversation
never let them see you
sweat they
never let them in

The sun shone for 10
years.
She was lost to all...

Masterpiece

I am an unfinished
masterpiece
      pencil strokes,
eraser marks, and
      a few ink stains.
Lyrics constantly
rearranged.
Trying to find that song I
wanna sang.

Painting on an empty
canvas.
Using brushes made of
angel wings.
Dipped in the blood of
Jesus.
My colors rich, deep, and
true.

The melody of my soul
as yet unsung.
All the words and notes
are here.

Waiting to be composed,
       for the greater
purpose.
A song to be sung until
the heavens
       weep and rejoice.

I am an unfinished
masterpiece
       pencil strokes,
eraser marks, and a
       few ink stains.
Lyrics constantly
rearranged.
Trying to find that song I
wanna sang...

Where We Stand

We stood in the land of
sheer natural beauty
Where our Mother holds
diamonds in her mines
Stolen from home
To stand on untamed
soil
We stood for our
heritage till
    it was teased, hated,
and forced
    away from us
We stand by and watch
our brothers and
    sisters kill each
other
For the sake of style
For the sake of money
For the sake of street
corner fame
We stand knees weak as
water and see
    our sons slaughtered

We stand in
righteousness before
   justice;
Pleading to be heard
But justice is blind...
She sees us not...
For she was never meant
   acknowledge us
She was blindfolded and
her scales
   weighted
We stand in refreshed
realization that
   this country was not
built for us
Although we built this
country
We stand before this
justice system
   hands held aloft
before us
Pleading for the
constitutional rights
   afforded us all

Except.....

MAGIC INK

All men are not seen
equal
   Justice and Liberty
are not for all

Where we stand
   is on the shoulders
of God

Where we stand
   is in self discovery

Where we stand
   is as Kings and
Queens

Where we stand
   is on the edge of
war

Where we stand
   is in our tomorrow!!!

Stars in Your Eyes

Because I see stars in
your eyes
       I see infinite
possibilities
I feel timeless occasions
upon us
Time stops for me
So not to rush my star
gazing
In your iris I see celestial
beings dancing
If I let go;
I could lose myself in
your eyes
I can make out,
       Ursa Major and Ursa
Minor
The wild and
unpredictable nature of
you
I keep looking,
slightly askew,
but deeper

MAGIC INK

I see Orion's Belt
Your warrior status,
Strength and reliability
Closing my eyes doesn't
obscure my sight
Holding your ink stained
mind in my hands
Searching for the source
of you
The Big Dipper is in the
fountain of your
knowledge
I drink from the Little
Dipper tasting your
intellect
Gaining insight

Do you see my stars??

Hands

Your hands on my hands
My hands on you
Your fingers caress my
skin as if,
    it was warm silk
Warm smooth waves of
passion form
      a knot in the bowels
of my stomach
Passion multiplies
And threatens to explode
and devour every
conscious thought
Yet your melodious
digits still create
sonnets
While tracing
      every curve
    and outline
       every dip
Your capable hands

MAGIC INK

These beautiful
instruments that take
pen to paper
Causing verbal art
   to turn white sand
    into a rainbow
As they cascade across
my secret treasures
Theses same artist tools
That work me into an
animalistic mindset
And lock my heart in a
cage
Where logic does not
exist
     and my body
surrenders
To your command
As I crumble in your
palms
Lift me to heights of
ecstasy that
     causes my body to
spasm in
     delight

A kingdom where your
hands wield magic
Which my heart beats to
a series of
      exhausting moans
The moans evolve into
shallow breaths
And the breaths
transform into a final
petition...
Of pleading and...
Needing...
you...
to...
touch...
me....
With those magic hands...

AGAIN...

Dream Connection

Walking a tightrope
between
  wakefulness and
slumber's surrender
A feat I rarely achieve
Longing for the soft
caress of the
  Sandman's touch
The day's events
swirling around in my
    mind
Future events not letting
me finish
  processing preceding
thoughts
Shakespeare wrote " To
sleep perchance
  to dream: Aye, there's
the rub"
The rub being, I gotta
sleep to dream of
  you

Dreaming: the release of
metal energies
  acquired during
waking hours
For in my dreams I have
a connection
  to you
Another place our minds
can meet
Paper to paper
Quill to quill
Noun to noun
Verb to verb
We can match wit with no
boundaries
No barriers
The distance between us
is simply
  thought away
Here in my dream
I see you for who you are
A walking breathing
poem
Ink runs through your
veins

MAGIC INK

Words cover your
feelings
So your emotions are
pure floetry
I see you here
In your purest form
So here I can be me
Perfectly imperfect
Dressed in my ideas
Gliding on wings of
knowledge
I seek you here
For here I know we
complete each other
Reaching our pinnacle
Here we can lose time
And gain so much more

until...
                    I wake...
Let me write this down
before my
    dream fades

Meeting Me

Sitting here listening to
your Ink
    flowing from your
paper
    to speaker
    in ear
    over mind
    irreparable damage to
my heart
Poetic flow the only balm
    life in rhyme
    love in lines
    pain in writes
    sex on smooth floetry
Letting my blood spill for
the sake of ink
Filling sheets of
parchment with my
    quill
Assuring my legacy in
those with like
    minds

MAGIC INK

Leaving cultivation
instructions for my
   seeds
Expressing my deeper
desires
   unknown to my
conscious self
Revealing my character
to my morals
Wondering if the two can
meet on
   mutual ground
Reintroducing myself to
me through
   poetry
So, as you get to know
my inner mind
Know we are all meeting
each other
   for the first time..

Black Woman

What makes me a black
woman?
Is it solely the color of
my skin?
The texture of my hair??
The way I carry my
curves?
My resolve to raise Kings
and Queens??
Is it the work I put in to
let my black
   brothers know they are
worthy??
Can it be the way I fight
to be seen
   for my true worth?
It is all these things, plus
so many
   more...

   I am a Black Woman

And I am Essential...

I Need You

The power you hold over
me...
I can't shake the need
you fill
   me with
I try to concentrate on
anything else
   and I come write back
to you
You overwhelm my mind
Warming my heart
And fueling my soul
Aggravating me to no
end
Yet, I yearn for you all
the time
You're like a drug
I feel you flow in my
veins
Making me high
Reinventing myself
constantly within
   your grasp

I can be myself with you
in my life
Show you what God has
done in my life
But, be so mischievous
you'll swear the
   devil is in me
Be sensual and seductive
Or, just get straight to it
and get nasty
   with you
And all the while your
willing to let
   anybody and
everybody see...
Neither of us care what
they think
But, truthfully I like it if
they enjoy what
   they see and get into
it...
You know all my deepest
secrets
So, never leave me
We've only been together
for a few

months
But, I want a lifetime with
you
Can't sleep because of
you
And when I do
I call out your name.....

Poetry...

Sweet Poetry

Tainted

I want to be tainted by
you
You already contaminate
my thoughts
I want you to adulterate
my body
Corrupt my sexuality
Destroy my inhibitions
I wanna go down on the
dark side of
   passion
Bound by your
imagination
Dominated by your
attention
Submit to your intent

You were Made for This

**Pushing through when
circumstances
  seem impossible
Fighting when flight
would be easier
Breathe easy
Although your head is
underwater**

Go farther

Dive deeper

**You were made for this
There's the Light
Reach for your source of
strength
Swim through
Make breakers in the
ocean of life
Your breakers can be
waves for**

others to surf
Be that force
Breathe deep
Dive in
Swim

You were made for this

Conversation

Connecting on another
level
Minds clicking into
places previously
left untouched
Desires being dated with
words shared
from an inner reservoir,
often ignored
Verbal massage given to
stimulate the
cerebral cortex
Releasing endorphins to
help cultivate the firing
of the erotic synopsis in
the brain
The connection of the
brain to the body's
response is undeniable
So, continue to enrich my
mind
And flood my system
with.....
Conversation

Untitled

**Breathing life into
my heavy heart
Your kiss is a
renewal
Your love a new
beginning
You are my sun
The future in the
horizon**

Hooked

I'm having a hard time
explaining to
myself
Why I'm hooked
Is it the words you spit?
The lines that leak from
your pen
I admit I'm hooked
Whether it's the sparkle
in your eye
Or mischief in your mind
Being hooked is gonna
get me caught
up
Thinking about your
hands
And that smile
Maybe being hooked
isn't so bad
But I'm sure it's not
going to end well
Yearning for the kisses
you share with

another
Wanting the caresses
you give such
explicit detail about
Now I know how a fish
feels
That hook is a bitch to
get off of.....

Strong Enough

Can you handle a
binding?
What about being
blindfolded?
Are you strong enough
to be bound
and blindfolded?
Are you strong enough
to handle the
anticipation?
Are you ready to be
assaulted by your
senses?
Can you do what your
told?
Ignore your bodies
natural responses?
Do not moan, even when
those feelings
take hold...
Can you be still??
Do not move!!

With desires building to
the point
of your spill....
Are you strong enough?
Never knowing when the
next touch
will be..
Anxious as to how it will
be delivered...
Are you strong enough
to beat down your
instinct??
To control your needs...
No arching of your back...
No moaning
Are you strong enough??
No begging for
satisfaction...
Are you strong enough?
To hold back....
To hold on....
Until you're told...

MAGIC INK

Cum...

Are you strong enough to surrender???

Raindrops

That moment when
raindrops slide
effortlessly down
the window
Destination unknown

Free of any
misconceptions
No ulterior motive
Another moment
Another raindrop
Until moments and
raindrops are
countless and
untimely

Watching a raindrop
slide effortlessly
down the window
Reality beckoning

MAGIC INK

Watch teardrops slide
effortlessly
down your face

Kiss Me

Kiss me softly where
your lips scarcely
touch mine
Cover my eyes so one
sense is lost
but another is
heightened
Kiss my ear so I feel your
life's
breathe warm next to
my skin
Kiss my neck so streams
of liquid
heat course down my
spine
Kiss my breast so you
feel each
heartbeat beneath
your lips
Kiss my stomach as it
intensifies
my hunger for you

MAGIC INK

Kiss my silken treasure
so my
juices flow freely

Kiss me

and

I'll kiss you back

Sands of Time

Through the sands of
time Love has
endured and been the
foundation of
Life
In every theological
prose love is the
basis of life
It's also the excuse for
harrowing strife
Love of money, power,
and/or a woman
has ignited or inflamed
countless
wars
It is said love is a many
splendid thing
Songs are written to
honor it
Poems are recited to
ensnare one's heart
For every passing
minute
Every grain of sand

MAGIC INK

Love is used for good or
bad
The word itself has lost
all structure
The emotion is used to
imprison
someone else's
thoughts and actions
Sands of time are course
and unyielding
Stripping the meaning
and intention
off of the emotional
revelations we
are next to experience
But know love never
changed
Over time love stayed
true
Our view was distorted
and
twisted
But as nature often does
she
produced gems from
the pressures

Black Sapphire

of life and death
Those gems have been
polished and
refined by the Sands of
Time
Time continues on
Grain by grain
Moment by moment
You are a gem

Addiction

Does anyone know the
precise moment
that addiction starts?
I just know this...
I need to hear your voice
I live for the moment you
touch me
skin to skin
I start to shake when you
whisper my
name
I can't hold still...
when you stroll
through my secret
garden
Hitting my system like a
sonic boom
Coursing through my
veins...
feeling liquid
fiyah...burning me from
inside out

Black Sapphire

I beg for more with every
thrust
To ride that sensual
wave of pleasure
up the mountain and
jump off the
cliff of ecstasy into
oblivion...

ad • dic • tion - noun -
The fact or condition
of being addicted to a
particular
substance, thing, or
activity

I may need rehab..

maybe not...

This is me

I'm a collection
Bits of information
Constant reclassification
I'm an em-path
My feelings strong and
true
I love and I love hard
I often love wrong
You'll never know when
my heart is
broken
For I'll always share my
smile
I'm a knowledge seeker
My first and most
enduring passion
are words
This will be my undoing

This is me
Love me or leave me
alone

Loving a Poet

I met your mind first
Sensual thoughts put on
paper
Embossed with liquid
fire
Singeing my cortex with
subliminal
messages of promised
released
Reading your lines
Peeking through the
windows of your
soul
Finding inspiration in
your angst
Finding solace in your
pain
Finding desire in your
determination
Your life printed before
me
Watching you manifest
in black and

MAGIC INK

white
Wondering who broke
your heart
What marked your spirit
In awe I watch you, I
listen,
You stand before me
speaking
the words,
I've read so often
Now they take on
another dimension
There is a new energy to
every
line
Substance to every
pause
Watching your lips form
the art that
is now second skin to me
Your voice caresses my
inner sanctum
I see your soul exposed
and open to
interpretation

Black Sapphire

**Your ink red from the
blood of loss, love, and
life
Your Ink found me.**

I'm loving this Poet...

The Classic Chase

I won't chase you
But you will give in
Begging will never be an
option
And you'll keep
returning
Games I'll never resort to
Surely you will enjoy
playing with me
Once your caught
You'll be completely
ensnared
Mental stimulation
co-existing with physical
amusement
Now we've stepped into
a metaphysical
plain
Where my lines enthrall
your heart
Words enchant your soul
My mentality beguiles
your body
The chase can be fun.....

Black Sapphire

Being captured will be...

Magnificent

**Rendez-moi, la chasse
est terminée**

**(surrender to me, the
chase is over)**

Writing

That feeling you get
when you just can't
deal with fake
smiles and hollow
laughs
Tears are close to the
surface and your
not sure why
You have a piece
missing and it's just
out of reach....

I look to the
sky.....close my eyes
and bleed
my pain through my
Ink

Recognizing My Poet

I wear many hats
I am a engineer by
necessity
I've built a dam that was
impenetrable
Plenty went in
Nothing was let out
I am a collector
Holding knowledge for
redemption at a
later date
Walking my path, I met a
couple of
demolition experts
They told me although
my dam was
well built, it had leaks
See, some of my
collections had seeped
through, and they saw
potential in my
apprehension
I was assured this was a
big job,

but must be done
They proceeded to tear
down walls
that took years to erect
Fears were resurrected
Hidden jewels
discovered
Another avenue paved
Now there is not a day
that my river doesn't run
free with:
Memories...
Dreams...
Ideas...
Desires....

All are fueling my quill
Recognizing my poet
was a job well
worth the endeavor

Memories

Memories have a span of
their own
They have different hues
Some are vivid
Some are faded
We are living memories
Mostly memories of love
shared
abandoned
neglected
rejoiced in
I can remember the first
time you spoke
to me
The first kiss
The first touch
I remember the first time
I surrendered to
you completely
And every time there
after
But...

MAGIC INK

I don't have any memory
of why we
argued
Why we yelled such
hurtful things
I remember the hurt
I remember the rain...
the stabbing pain
I have the memory of you
walking
away

Love Me like Africa

Love me like the gazelle
sure and graceful
Love me like the giraffe
seeing above and
beyond my faults
Love me like the hyena
keep me smiling and
laughing
Love me like the lion
with righteousness
and leadership
Love me like the African
landscape
unrelenting and
daunting
Love me like the African
sun
hot and everlasting
Love me like the African
mines
for there is a gem
inside
Love me like the African
people

MAGIC INK

with loyalty and whole
heartedly

Love me like Mother
Africa

For I am she..

A Tanka Style Poem

I often give it
It's my turn to swallow it
A spoonful of sugar...
Naw
Two more shots of Skyy
Vodka
That jagged little
pill...Damn

** a tanks poem consists
of**
5 lines
1st line 5 syllables
2nd line 7 syllables
3rd line 5 syllables
4th line 7 syllables
5th line 7 syllables

Matrix

A mere walk is not a walk
It's a journey
A drink of water is...
a life saving method of
libation
ingestion
To touch ones heart is
Persona non grata

Here in the Matrix
life is granted to the
useful
Love is not useful
It brings happiness,
hope, and dreams
What use do we have for
that in the

Matrix??

Everything is
asymmetrical

Chaos is the creed of this
nation
Fear, intolerance, and
desolation is
what we nurture you
with
So give up, let go I'll
control all
Come in and be prepared
for
everlasting suffering

Welcome to the Matrix

One More

I want one more
glance

touch

whisper

Leave me with a
note

wink

kiss

Take with you this
solitude

desolation

pain

One more moment
in time..

It's all I ask..

About the Author

Kristi grew up in small town Oklahoma where friends were family and family was forever.

Writing was introduced to her as a form of therapy after her mother passed away when Kristi was 10 years-old, but eventually writing took a back seat to life, and all its real challenges.

Writing again resurfaced when she began writing lyrics for the melodies her husband created. Severely self conscious of her writing, it was years before she allowed it to make its public appearance at the urging of family and friends.

Through the Facebook poetry community and her quickly growing fan base, Kristi is still learning to love her pen...

"I am loving my journey on this path..." **Black Sapphire**

MAGIC INK

Kristi"*BlackSapphire*"McGee

www.ingramcontent.com/pod-product-compliance
Lightning Source LLC
Chambersburg PA
CBHW060714030426
42337CB00017B/2859